DOLPHINS
A First Look

PERCY LEED

GRL Consultants,
Diane Craig and Monica Marx,
Certified Literacy Specialists

Lerner Publications ◆ Minneapolis

Educator Toolbox

Reading books is a great way for kids to express what they're interested in. Before reading this title, ask the reader these questions:

What do you think this book is about? Look at the cover for clues.

What do you already know about dolphins?

What do you want to learn about dolphins?

Let's Read Together

Encourage the reader to use the pictures to understand the text.

Point out when the reader successfully sounds out a word.

Praise the reader for recognizing sight words such as *they* and *are*.

TABLE OF CONTENTS

Dolphins 4

You Connect! 21

STEM Snapshot 22

Photo Glossary 23

Learn More 23

Index 24

Dolphins

Dolphins are ocean animals. They live in oceans around the world.

flippers

Most dolphins are gray.
They have two flippers.
Their tails are called flukes.

fluke

Dolphins breathe
air through a
blowhole.
It is on top
of the head.

blowhole

Why do you think the blowhole is on top of the head?

Dolphins play.
They jump out
of the water.
They swim in the waves.

Many dolphins
live in groups
called pods.
Pods swim together.

**Why do you think
dolphins live in pods?**

A pod hunts
together too.

Dolphins catch fish.
They also catch squid.

Dolphins make sounds. The sounds hit their food and bounce back to the dolphins. This tells them where the food is.

sound
waves

food

17

Dolphins are mammals.
Their babies grow
inside them.

A dolphin baby stays with its mother.
It grows and learns.

You Connect!

What is something you like about dolphins?

Have you ever seen video of dolphins swimming?

What other ocean animals do you know about?

STEM Snapshot

Encourage students to think and ask questions like scientists. Ask the reader:

What is something you learned about dolphins?

What is something you noticed about dolphin babies?

What is something you still want to learn about dolphins?

Photo Glossary

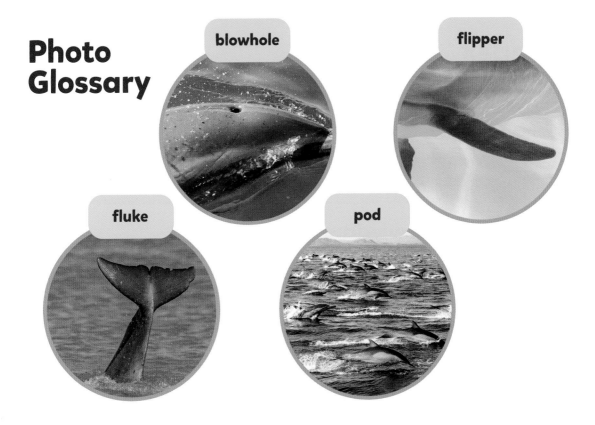

blowhole

flipper

fluke

pod

Learn More

Bassier, Emma. *Dolphins*. Minneapolis: Pop!, 2020.

Leaf, Christina. *Dolphins*. Minneapolis: Bellwether Media, 2021.

Schuh, Mari C. *Dolphins*. Minneapolis: Jump!, 2022.

Index

babies, 18, 20
blowhole, 8, 9

flippers, 7
flukes, 7

pods, 12, 13, 14
sounds, 16

Photo Acknowledgments

The images in this book are used with the permission of: © Andrea Izzotti/iStockphoto, pp. 16–17; © Binson Calfort/ Shutterstock Images, p. 15; © cookelma/iStockphoto, p. 10; © DavidMSchrader/iStockphoto, pp. 12–13, 23 (pod); © ersler/iStockphoto, pp. 6–7, 23 (flipper); © FourOaks/iStockphoto, pp. 10–11; © Harry Collins/iStockphoto, pp. 7, 23 (fluke); © Joost van Uffelen/Shutterstock Images, p. 20; © Michelle de Villiers/iStockphoto, pp. 4–5; © Stéphane ROCHON/iStockphoto, pp. 14, 18–19; © triggerfishsaul/iStockphoto, pp. 8–9, 23 (blowhole).

Cover Photo: © Andrea Izzotti/Shutterstock Images

Design Elements: © Mighty Media, Inc.

Copyright © 2023 by Lerner Publishing Group, Inc.

Lerner Publications Company
An imprint of Lerner Publishing Group, Inc.
241 First Avenue North
Minneapolis, MN 55401 USA

For reading levels and more information, look up this title at www.lernerbooks.com.

Main body text set in Mikado a Medium.
Typeface provided by Hannes von Doehren.

Library of Congress Cataloging-in-Publication Data

Names: Leed, Percy, 1968- author.
Title: Dolphins : a first look / Percy Leed ; GRL consultants, Diane Craig and Monica Marx, Certified Literacy Specialists.
Description: Minneapolis : Lerner Publications, [2023] | Series: Read about ocean animals (read for a better world) | Includes bibliographical references and index. | Audience: Ages 5-8 | Audience: Grades K-1 | Summary: "Dolphins are some of the most playful creatures in the sea. Simple text and engaging photos introduce readers to these social ocean animals"— Provided by publisher.
Identifiers: LCCN 2021051292 (print) | LCCN 2021051293 (ebook) | ISBN 9781728459110 (library binding) | ISBN 9781728464152 (paperback) | ISBN 9781728461700 (ebook)
Subjects: LCSH: Dolphins—Juvenile literature.
Classification: LCC QL737.C432 L436 2023 (print) | LCC QL737. C432 (ebook) | DDC 599.53—dc23/eng/20211021

LC record available at https://lccn.loc.gov/2021051292
LC ebook record available at https://lccn.loc.gov/2021051293

Manufactured in the United States of America
1 – CG – 7/15/22